WITHDRAWN

Published in 2015 by The Rosen Publishing Group, Inc.
29 East 21st Street, New York, NY 10010

Photo Credits: **KEY** tl=top left; tc=top center; tcr=top center right; tr=top right; c=center; bl=bottom left; bc=bottom center; bcr=bottom center right; br=bottom right; bg=background

CBT = Corbis; DT = Dreamstime; GI = Getty Images;
iS = istockphoto.com; PS = Photoshot; SH = Shutterstock; TPL = photolibrary.com

Coverc CBT; **2-3**bg CBT; **6-7**bg DT; **7**c iS; **8**bg GI; tl iS; bc PS; **9**bc, tc SH; **11**tc CBT; **14**bl CBT; **15**br iS; **15-16**tc SH; **19**tr SH; **20**tr iS; **20-21**bl iS; **22**bl SH; **23**tr SH; **29**br CBT; tl DT; cr TPL

All illustrations copyright Weldon Owen Pty Ltd, except **20-21**c Magic Group.
16tl; **20**tl; **22**tl; **24**tl Andrew Davies/Creative Communication; **22**br; **23**bl, br Gary Hanna

WELDON OWEN PTY LTD
Managing Director: Kay Scarlett
Creative Director: Sue Burk
Publisher: Helen Bateman
Senior Vice President, International Sales: Stuart Laurence
Vice President Sales North America: Ellen Towell
Administration Manager, International Sales: Kristine Ravn

Library of Congress Cataloging-in-Publication Data

Einspruch, Andrew, author.
 Migration : animals on the move / By Andrew Einspruch.
    pages cm. — (Discovery education. Animals)
 Includes index.
 ISBN 978-1-4777-6948-5 (library binding) — ISBN 978-1-4777-6949-2 (pbk.) —
ISBN 978-1-4777-6950-8 (6-pack)
 1. Animal migration—Juvenile literature. 2. Migratory animals—Juvenile literature. 3. Animal behavior—Juvenile literature. I. Title.
 QL754.E46 2015
 591.56'8—dc23
                           2013047560

Manufactured in the United States of America

CPSIA Compliance Information: Batch #WS14PK3: For Further Information contact Rosen Publishing, New York, New York at 1-800-237-9932

3 9957 00186 3592

Discovery
EDUCATION™

MIGRATION
ANIMALS ON THE MOVE

ANDREW EINSPRUCH

PowerKiDS
press™

New York

Contents

Why Migrate?

Animals in the wild migrate for a number of reasons. Some follow the seasons, seeking more pleasant places to be before the weather changes. Others follow food, which is either on the move itself, or is more plentiful somewhere else due to the season. If cold weather, a drought, or a population explosion dries up the food supply, then animals get moving to look for other food to eat.

Still other animals migrate to find a mate and reproduce. They choose a place that might have a particular kind of food available, or is protected so that they can produce offspring in safety.

Zebras
Every year, hundreds of thousands of zebras cross almost 2,000 miles (3,200 km) as they take part in one of Earth's most spectacular migrations. They travel in a continuous clockwise direction, looking for fresh grass and water through Tanzania and Kenya.

Canada geese

Canada geese migrate twice yearly: in spring and then in fall. They are known for the distinctive V-shaped pattern they form when flying, which helps them conserve energy. If the wind is right, these geese can fly more than 1,500 miles (2,400 km) in just 24 hours.

Types of migration

Animals migrate in different ways. Some go back and forth. Others only go, and they do not come back. It depends on how long they live, and the reasons they are on the move.

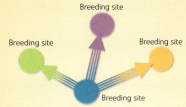

One-way migration

In a one-way migration, a group of animals moves to live somewhere new. This is often seen in insects, such as ants and bees.

Nomadic migration

Nomadic migration sees animals breeding at several places during their lives. A particular species, such as budgerigars or zebra finches, may return to a given location only when conditions (such as rainfall) are just right.

Return migration

Return migration is the kind most people know. Animals, such as Canada geese, spend part of the year in one place and part in another, and predictably go back and forth between them.

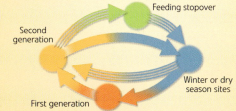

Migration circuits

Migration circuits are like return migration, but with extra stops along the way and in a pattern that never ends. The migration of zebras and wildebeest are a circuit migration.

July–August

In July, the herds cross the often dangerous Grumeti River. Those that do not drown or are not taken by crocodiles continue into Kenya for the lush plains of the Lamai Wedge and the Mara Triangle. There, the Mara River presents another dangerous obstacle the herds must cross.

KENYA
TANZANIA

Mara

MASAI MARA
NATIONAL
RESERVE

September–October

August

November

July

Grumeti

June

SERENGETI
NATIONAL
PARK

Mbalageti

May

December

April

Serengeti
Plain

Lake Ndutu

January–March

April–May

In a spectacular display of animal movement, the herds travel west and north through frequent rain toward the western Serengeti's grassy plains and woodlands. As the rains taper off in June, the wildebeest mate.

January–March

At this time of year, the wildebeest are in the Serengeti Plains and the Ngorongoro Conservation Area. During the three weeks around the start of February, mothers give birth to their calves. This is a dangerous time, attracting the interest of lions.

September–December
The Mara Plains are home to large herds from September. By November, it is time to head back south to the Serengeti and Ngorongoro, where the mothers will eventually give birth again.

Mating rivals
The wildebeest mate while in the western Serengeti Plains. Males compete for the chance to mate with the choicest females.

Wildebeest

Each year, more than 1 million wildebeest, or gnus, make the great migration across part of Africa. Their 1,800-mile (2,900-km) journey goes through Tanzania's Serengeti Plains, Kenya's Masai Mara National Reserve, down to Tanzania's Ngorongoro Conservation Area, and back again. They travel in a constant clockwise cycle, varying the path slightly depending on the season and conditions.

The wildebeest travel with zebras and ostriches. Wildebeest have good hearing, but not very good sight or smell. Ostriches have good eyes, while zebras have a keen sense of smell. Each takes cues from the others, helping them all to be aware of predators.

Humpbacks

Humpback whales are massive, graceful creatures that journey across half of Earth, from north to south. They mate and give birth in the warmer water found toward the equator. They then travel toward the poles where their food supply (krill) lives.

Humpback breaching

In an amazing motion known as breaching, humpback whales hurl themselves most of the way out of the water, turn half a circle, and then fall back to the water on their back, making a loud slapping sound. Scientists think breaching is communication, possibly a warning or a way to let other whales know they are there.

Whales

Not all migration takes place on land. Plenty of it happens in the oceans, and whales are a perfect example. Similar to many migratory birds, whales can travel several thousands of miles (km) every year. They move to find conditions that are suited to them, be it a place to find their preferred kind of food or to mate.

As warm-blooded mammals, whales are sensitive to the water temperature around them. Changes in temperature due to the seasons cause them to move from one part of the ocean to another. The seasons also affect food supplies, which decrease in cold, winter weather.

Southern rights
Although they do not travel as far as humpbacks, Southern right whales still move thousands of miles (km) each year. Like other whales, Southern rights were hunted to the brink of extinction by the mid-1800s, and populations dropped from 100,000 to around 4,000. These whales have been protected since 1937, but, even so, their numbers are nowhere close to full recovery.

Migration routes
Whales move across the ocean, using paths that are as predictable as those chosen by land animals and birds. They tend not to cross the equator, staying, instead, in the hemisphere (north or south) of their birth.

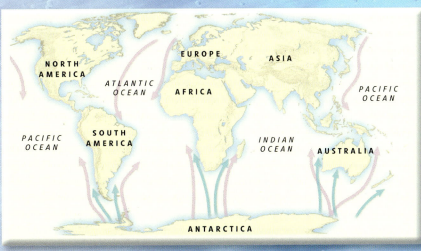

KEY Southern right whale   Humpback whale

Dragonflies

Of the 400 or so dragonfly species in North America, scientists think only around 12 migrate. Scientists tagged dragonflies with radio transmitters, and their research showed that, in fall, these particular dragonflies head south. They travel from the northern US and southern Canada to Mexico, the Caribbean, and the southern US. Their offspring make the return trip in spring.

Locusts and Other Bugs

Locusts are a kind of grasshopper that is known for forming massive swarms every now and then that sweep across the land, devouring all plant life in their path. A swarming locust can eat its weight in plant material every day. With millions of locusts packed together in the swarm, the results are nothing less than devastating, especially to farms and food sources, as the locusts move from place to place in search of somewhere to satisfy their insatiable need for food.

Locust swarms can cover hundreds of miles (km) and can tower almost a mile (1.6 km) into the air. Up in the air, winds carry them along until gravity pulls them back to Earth, helping them migrate.

MORE BUGS THAT MIGRATE

Grasshopper

Leafhopper

A form of Californian ladybug lives in valleys. In summer, however, the month-old adults migrate to the Sierra Mountains. Similarly, grasshoppers and leafhoppers move from place to place.

Ladybug

Forming a swarm
Locusts normally live solitary lives. However, if conditions are right (such as good rainfall), their numbers increase. As they swarm, their bodies change—they develop black and yellow patterns, their shoulders broaden, and their wings lengthen.

ARCTIC

KEY

→ Route taken

AFRICA

Breeding grounds

Arctic terns breed across a wide area near the Arctic, including Canada, Alaska, Iceland, Greenland, and Russia. When it starts getting too cold, they head south to the Antarctic, where the warmer weather means more food will be available.

SOUTH AMERICA

Record holders

In 2005, scientists using tracking tags found that sooty shearwaters clock up to 40,000 miles (64,000 km), twice the distance they thought Arctic terns traveled. But new tagging research from 2010 showed that Arctic terns were still the migration champions, almost doubling the shearwater's recorded movements.

Pairing up
Male and female Arctic terns remain mates for life. They have elaborate courtship rituals, including particular flying behaviors and offers of food.

Arctic Terns

The Arctic tern is one of the world's great travelers. This amazing bird weighs just over 3.5 ounces (100 g), has a 15-inch (38-cm) body, and wings that span 31 inches (79 cm). Yet, each year, it crosses the length of the globe twice. The round-trip covers as many as 50,000 miles (80,000 km), going from the Arctic to the Antarctic and back.

Arctic terns enjoy two summers every year, and see more daylight annually than any other animal. They live for around 34 years, which means that, in a lifetime, they travel about 1.5 million miles (2.4 million km). That is enough mileage for three round-trips to the moon.

Feeding time
Fish is on the menu for Arctic terns. They hunt by hovering over the ocean waters, then plunging in to nab their meal.

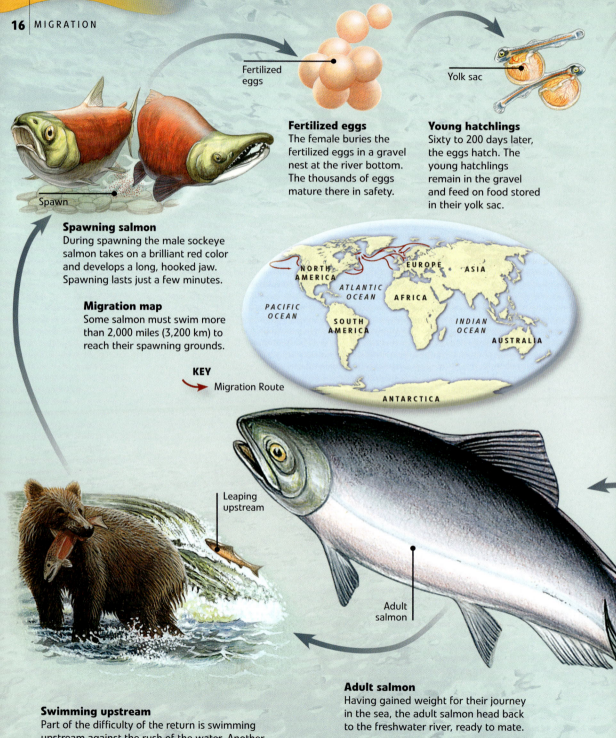

Fertilized eggs

Yolk sac

Fertilized eggs
The female buries the fertilized eggs in a gravel nest at the river bottom. The thousands of eggs mature there in safety.

Young hatchlings
Sixty to 200 days later, the eggs hatch. The young hatchlings remain in the gravel and feed on food stored in their yolk sac.

Spawn

Spawning salmon
During spawning the male sockeye salmon takes on a brilliant red color and develops a long, hooked jaw. Spawning lasts just a few minutes.

Migration map
Some salmon must swim more than 2,000 miles (3,200 km) to reach their spawning grounds.

NORTH AMERICA

EUROPE

ASIA

ATLANTIC OCEAN

AFRICA

PACIFIC OCEAN

SOUTH AMERICA

INDIAN OCEAN

AUSTRALIA

KEY
Migration Route

ANTARCTICA

Leaping upstream

Adult salmon

Swimming upstream
Part of the difficulty of the return is swimming upstream against the rush of the water. Another difficulty is avoiding predators such as bears.

Adult salmon
Having gained weight for their journey in the sea, the adult salmon head back to the freshwater river, ready to mate.

Fry

Fry
The young salmon, called fry, wriggle out of the gravel and into the stream.

Young salmon

Young salmon
Some fry head for the sea almost immediately. Others wait and grow for a few weeks, a year, or as long as five years before heading downriver.

The Life Cycle of Salmon

Smolting
Smolting is a process that changes the salmon's body so it can live in salt water.

S almon migrate over a period of years. Born in freshwater rivers, they make their way to sea. One to eight years later, they make a long and dangerous return to the exact waters of their birth, where they spawn and start the next generation.

Pacific salmon typically die after they spawn, while Atlantic salmon normally swim back to sea, and make the journey again a few years later.

Smolt

Killer whale

Living in the sea

Salmon out at sea
Salmon live in the sea for some years, growing and preparing for their arduous return journey.

Predators
In the sea, salmon face dangers from predators including fish, birds, seals, and whales.

Elephants

Elephants typically walk several miles (km) daily, and can walk as many as 50 miles (80 km) in a single day. They are built to move around. Even though their bodies cannot gallop or jump, they can hit a top speed of 25 miles (40 km) per hour as they go from place to place.

How much they migrate depends on where they live. Jungle elephants typically have plenty of food around them, so they do not need to travel as far. Elephants living in less rich environments, such as savannas or plains, must cover more ground to find the food they need, especially in the dry times.

Feet first

Elephant feet are well suited for the walking they do. They are round and have three, four, or five nails, depending on the breed of elephant. A pad underneath cushions the impact. When elephants shift their weight onto a particular foot, the foot swells. When they shift off it, the foot shrinks again. This helps to prevent them from getting stuck in mud.

MIGRATING THROUGH THE SEASONS

Elephants move differently depending on the seasons. In the wet season, when mating and birthing occur, elephants range widely toward savannas and grasslands. In dry times, they cluster closer together around lakes, waterholes, swamps, and bogs. When elephants find water, they slurp up around 26 gallons (100 l) every day. For an adult elephant, that is about seven trunks full.

Elephants by a waterhole

That's Amazing!

During migration, each family is led by a matriarch, who might be as old as 70. She helps the group remember the best places to eat and drink across hundreds of square miles (sq km).

Sea Turtles

All female turtles leave water to find a place on land where they can lay their eggs. Some just wander over to a nearby stream bank. However, all female sea turtles migrate to go back to the spot where they were born. This trip can cover hundreds of miles (km). The female ends up on a beach or farther inland, where she digs a hole and lays her eggs.

Turtles are not exactly doting mothers. Once they lay their eggs, the females head back to the water, leaving the eggs to hatch by themselves. When the babies are born, they are on their own.

A dangerous journey
Baby green turtles dig their way up to the sand's surface, then often wait for dark to rush to the sea so they can avoid land predators such as crabs. In the water, they must avoid sharks and other threats.

Courtship and mating
Male sea turtles mate with females in the sea. Courtship rituals include neck biting, head nuzzling, or perhaps biting the rear flippers. If the female responds, mating takes place over the next six or so hours. Two weeks after mating, the females are ready to make the trip to land.

Turtle life cycle

For male sea turtles, life is a one-way trip from land to sea. For females, however, long months in the sea are punctuated by short trips to land for laying eggs. Because they do not care for their young, female sea turtles produce many babies so that the odds of some surviving to adulthood are increased.

Laying eggs
Females go onto land, dig a hole, and bury their eggs.

Meeting
Males and females perform courtship rituals at breeding grounds in the ocean.

Mating
Females mate with multiple partners and store sperm to fertilize more than one set of eggs.

Growing up
Young turtles that make it to the ocean grow to maturity there.

Hatchlings
Baby turtles hatch, dig out of the sand, and head for water.

Digging deep
The female green turtle digs a 3-foot (1-m) hole in the beach for the 100 or so eggs she is about to lay. She wants to get deep enough so the temperature and moisture will be constant for her soft, leathery eggs. After she deposits them, she covers the eggs with sand, and heads back to sea, leaving them to incubate.

Butterflies and Moths

For such small and delicate animals, butterflies cover amazingly long distances. Like birds, butterflies take to the skies to find more favorable conditions—more food, better weather, or a good place to mate and lay eggs.

There is one big difference when compared to bird migration, however. Adult birds normally make a round-trip—they go and come back. Butterflies generally have much shorter lives, so they tend to go in one direction, while their offspring make it back to where they started. In fact, it can take several generations of butterflies to cover the territory needed to make a round-trip.

Painted lady

Other migrators
Numerous butterfly species are migratory, moving with the seasons. The painted lady takes advantage of favorable winds to head from Africa to Spain every year. Similarly, the cabbage butterfly flies a few hundred miles (km) on its yearly journey from the European continent to Britain. Butterflies are known to use the Sun to help them navigate.

KEY

- Eastern wintering ground
- Eastern summer grounds
- Western wintering grounds
- Western summer grounds

- Generation 1
- Generation 2
- Generation 3
- Generation 4

MOTHS

Bogong moth

Related to butterflies, moths also migrate. For example, Australia's bogong moth is famous for escaping the summer heat in the southeast of the country by flying to the Victorian Alps and the Snowy Mountains in New South Wales. They fly at night, and cluster in dark caves and crevices during the day.

Going the distance

Monarch butterflies can fly 50 miles (80 km) a day and can cover 3,100 miles (5,000 km) in total. Monarchs normally live for between two and six weeks, but those born in late summer live for much longer. They journey south to mountains near Mexico City and spend the winter there. In spring, they start a return trip, ultimately living for around eight months.

Eels

Like salmon, many eel species spend part of their lives in salt water and part of their lives in freshwater, making a migration between the two. European and American eels are famous for spawning in one particular place—the Sargasso Sea in the North Atlantic Ocean.

1 Spawning
Mature eels spawn in the ocean water of the Sargasso Sea. The eggs (and when they hatch, the larvae) drift northeast, carried by the Gulf Stream. This can last up to three years.

2 Juvenile eels
The larvae undergo significant changes. At first, juveniles are called glass eels because they are almost transparent. They slowly get pigment in the skin, and eventually swim into the freshwater of rivers as elvers, small versions of adult-form eels.

3 Adult lives
Adult eels stay in their freshwater homes for between 6 and 20 years. Here they mature and grow into what are called silver eels.

Gulf Stream

Canary Current

Range of European eel

Sargasso Sea spawning grounds

KEY
→ Cool Canary Current
→ Warm Gulf Stream

Strong currents
The Sargasso Sea is an interesting location because it has strong ocean currents surrounding it: the Gulf Stream, the North Atlantic Equatorial Current, the Canary Current, and the North Atlantic Current. These currents help the eels move around.

4 Migration
When they feel the urge to spawn, the silver eels head downriver toward the ocean. They cross the ocean without eating, relying solely on stored energy. When they reach the Sargasso Sea, they spawn and then die.

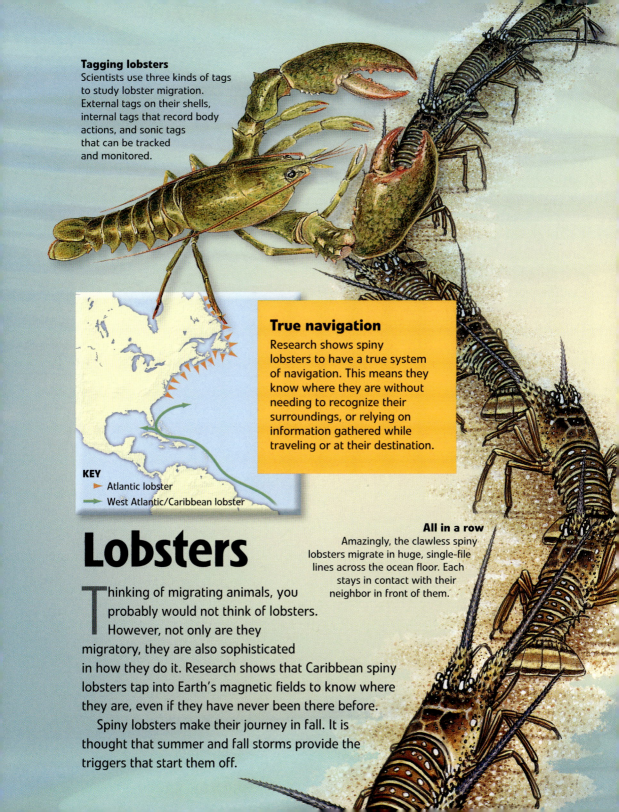

Tagging lobsters

Scientists use three kinds of tags to study lobster migration. External tags on their shells, internal tags that record body actions, and sonic tags that can be tracked and monitored.

True navigation

Research shows spiny lobsters to have a true system of navigation. This means they know where they are without needing to recognize their surroundings, or relying on information gathered while traveling or at their destination.

KEY
- ▶ Atlantic lobster
- ➤ West Atlantic/Caribbean lobster

All in a row

Amazingly, the clawless spiny lobsters migrate in huge, single-file lines across the ocean floor. Each stays in contact with their neighbor in front of them.

Lobsters

Thinking of migrating animals, you probably would not think of lobsters. However, not only are they migratory, they are also sophisticated in how they do it. Research shows that Caribbean spiny lobsters tap into Earth's magnetic fields to know where they are, even if they have never been there before.

Spiny lobsters make their journey in fall. It is thought that summer and fall storms provide the triggers that start them off.

Birds

Every year, all over the world, birds of all feathers take to the skies for their annual migrations. They take many different paths, some of which are complicated, and some of which are simple. A path from a particular breeding ground to a particular winter home is called a migration route. These routes cluster together to form general avian highways called flyways.

There are ten main flyways around the globe. Generally, they run north to south, and often follow natural formations, such as mountain ranges, river valleys, or coastlines. These provide places to stop, where the migrating birds can rest and eat.

Rufous hummingbird
This bird travels from Alaska to Mexico for winter, crossing the Rocky Mountains in July and August to enjoy the nectar from wildflowers.

Latham's snipe
This bird breeds in Japan, then travels to eastern Australia, spending Autumn on the southeastern coast and Tasmania.

ARCTIC OCEAN

NORTH AMERICA

ATLANTIC OCEAN

PACIFIC OCEAN

SOUTH AMERICA

Wandering albatross
With the largest wingspan of any bird, the wandering albatross flies the skies of the Southern Ocean. It can spend hours in the air without flapping its wings.

Short-tailed shearwater
Breeding in southeast Australia, this bird takes two migration journeys every year, one to the Pacific Ocean and one to the Antarctic.

White stork
The white stork takes advantage of thermals, rising columns of hot air, to fly from the Black Sea to the Mediterranean Sea. This soaring is an energy-efficient way to travel.

EUROPE

ASIA

AFRICA

AUSTRALIA

INDIAN OCEAN

SOUTHERN OCEAN

ANTARCTICA

Barn swallow
This very widely found bird breeds in North America, Europe and Northern Asia, and winters in South America, Africa, Southeast Asia, and northern Australia.

Eurasian teal
This commonly found duck breeds in many places across Europe and Asia. Marked with bright teal green markings, it flies from the Black Sea to the Mediterranean Sea in winter.

American kestrel
This small falcon flies from its breeding grounds across North America to its winter home in the south. Its flight path has no mountains in the way and has plenty of food and water.

Crossing the river
The great migration of zebras, ostriches, and wildebeest in Africa includes crossing two major rivers—the Grumeti and the Mara. In both places, crocodiles lie in wait, hoping to make a meal from a drinking or swimming animal.

Ground squirrel
The ground squirrel has many predators that make its occasional migrations dangerous. From the sky come eagles, kites, and hawks. It can also be attacked by coyotes, foxes, weasels, and badgers.

Dangers

Animals have to be careful if they want to survive. Migration means many animals are in the same place at the same time. While there is often safety in numbers, and being on the move can help, migration also means that these animals are tempting targets for those who prey on them.

Predators often know when and where animals travel and rest, and where they can best take advantage of any vulnerability. Or they might just follow alongside, looking for an unfortunate creature who falters or slips away from the group.

PANIC IN THE CROWD

Lemmings migrate when they experience a population explosion. What happens is that too many of them move at the same time, and cliffs, rivers, and boulders cause bottlenecks. Panicked lemmings start to flee, but they flee into danger.

Lemmings

Common toad
Despite having to migrate only 1 to 2 miles (1.6–3.2 km), the common toad's journey is a dangerous one. It must cross roads, and is often killed by vehicles. Each year, 22 tons (20 t) of toads are killed on British roads.

Glossary

breaching
(BREECH-ing) A movement some whales make where they thrust themselves out of the ocean water, turn half a circle, then fall back to the water on their back.

flyways
(FLY-wayz) Commonly used migration routes taken by migratory birds.

fry (FRY) Young salmon that have matured from hatchlings but are not yet fully matured salmon.

hatchlings
(HACH-lingz) The young of certain animals, such as salmon and turtles, that have just hatched from their eggs.

incubate
(IN-kyoo-bayt) To keep an egg warm until the baby inside is ready to hatch.

kestrel
(KEHS-trul) A type of falcon.

krill
(KRIL) A kind of shrimplike animal that humpback whales feed on.

locusts
(LOH-kusts) Kinds of grasshoppers known for swarming and devouring plant life.

mating
(MAY-ting) The coming together of the male and female of a species to produce young.

matriarch (MAY-tree-ark) An elderly female.

migration
(my-GRAY-shun) The natural movement of animals from one place to another.

migration route
(my-GRAY-shun ROOT) The lane of travel from a breeding ground to a wintering location used by migratory animals.

navigate
(NA-vuh-gayt) To guide an object purposefully from one place to another.

nomadic
(noh-MA-dik) Living a life of regular movement from one place to another.

pigment
(PIG-ment) The substance in an animal's skin that gives it color.

predator
(PREH-duh-ter) An animal that hunts another animal.

prey
(PRAY) An animal that is hunted by another animal.

smolting
(SMOL-ting) Changing, so a salmon can survive in salt water.

spawn
(SPAWN) To produce and deposit large quantities of eggs in the water. This reproductive method is used by animals such as fish and frogs.

sperm
(SPERM) The reproductive cells of males passed on during mating.

swarm
(SWORM) The spontaneous gathering of a large number of insects.

tern
(TURN) A type of slender bird similar to a gull.

thermals (THER-mulz) Rising columns of hot air.

transmitter
(trantst-MIH-ter) An electronic device that sends out a signal.

true navigation
(TROO na-vuh-GAY-shun) Being able to navigate without needing to recognize one's surroundings, or relying on information gathered while traveling to or from the destination.

warm-blooded
(WORM-bluh-did) Describes animals whose body maintains a constant temperature.

wildebeest
(WIL-deh-beest) A native African animal that is also called a gnu.

Index

Websites

Due to the changing nature of Internet links, PowerKids Press has developed an online list of websites related to the subject of this book. This site is updated regularly. Please use this link to access the list:
www.powerkidslinks.com/disc/move/